PAINTING WITH

BOB ROSS™
FOR KIDS

With these simple-to-follow lessons,
in no time you'll be painting just like television's
favorite painter, Bob Ross!

Hello, I'm Bob Ross, and I'd like to welcome you to *Painting with Bob Ross for Kids.* Certainly glad you could join us today. We're going to have a fantastic time, **so let's get started.**

BOB ROSS INC.

Walter Foster
Jr.

Quarto.com • WalterFoster.com

© 2023 Quarto Publishing Group USA Inc.
Text and images © 2023 Bob Ross Inc.
® Bob Ross name, images and other marks are registered trademarks of Bob Ross Inc.
© Bob Ross Inc. All rights reserved. Used with permission.

First Published in 2023 by Walter Foster Jr., an imprint of The Quarto Group,
100 Cummings Center, Suite 265-D, Beverly, MA 01915, USA.
T (978) 282-9590 **F** (978) 283-2742

Walter Foster Jr. titles are also available at discount for retail, wholesale, promotional, and bulk purchase. For details, contact the Special Sales Manager by email at specialsales@quarto.com or by mail at The Quarto Group, Attn: Special Sales Manager, 100 Cummings Center, Suite 265-D, Beverly, MA 01915, USA.

27 26 25 24 23   1 2 3 4 5

ISBN: 978-0-7603-8531-9

Library of Congress Cataloging-in-Publication Data available.

Printed in China

The Bob Ross for Kids™ brushes, knife, paints, basecoat, canvasboards, and the instructions in this book do not produce the same results you see Bob Ross do on his popular *Joy of Painting* show. This special kids' system is completely different, but still inspires creativity and great joy.

—Happy Painting!

TABLE OF CONTENTS

Welcome to Painting with Bob Ross for Kids!

Now you can paint the Bob Ross way with your own materials, just like television's favorite artist! We'll show you how to set up your painting studio, and then you can pick one of the paintings in this book and get started.

The lessons in this book are really easy to follow! Read each step carefully, and study the how-to pictures before you try it yourself. You'll see some helpful tips here and there too. A great looking painting is just a few minutes away!

When you're setting up to paint, start by covering your work station with newspaper or paper towels. Set up your canvas and the paint colors you will be using. Fill a disposable plastic cup with water. Next, carefully pour a small amount of each color you need onto your palette.

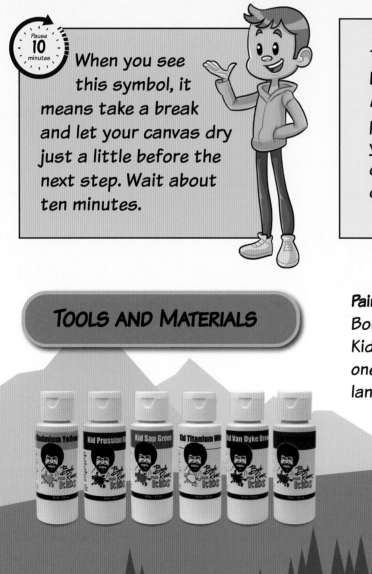

Pause 10 minutes

When you see this symbol, it means take a break and let your canvas dry just a little before the next step. Wait about ten minutes.

These Bob Ross Kid products can be purchased as part of the *Bob Ross for Kids: Happy Lessons in a Box* painting kit at **www.bobross.com** or at your favorite neighborhood arts and crafts store. You can also use any other water-based acrylic paints.

TOOLS AND MATERIALS

Paints
Bob carefully chose these colors in his Kid line because they work nicely with one another to create natural-looking landscapes with ease!

Cadmium Yellow · Kid Prussian Blue · Kid Sap Green · Kid Titanium White · Kid Van Dyke Brown

Paint Brushes

Bob's Kid synthetic-bristled brushes vary in size, shape, and texture. Carefully designed by Bob himself, many of the techniques you'll learn depend on how the paint is loaded onto these brushes. By following his instructions, you can create amazing effects on the canvas, just like him!

Here are the brushes used in this book:

Kid Background Brush used for painting larger areas.

Kid Landscape Brush used for applying Kid Liquid White, painting clouds, skies, water, trees, and bushes.

Kid Liner Brush used for sticks, twigs, limbs, and small details, including your signature!

Kid Fan Brush used for clouds, mountains, tree trunks, foothills, and grassy areas.

Kid Painting Knife used to mix colors, as well as for painting!

Brush and Station Cleaning

Make sure to clean your brushes after each use to keep them in good condition. Wash the brush and wipe dry with a soft cloth or paper towel. Keep paper towels or rags close to your station to clean your painting area as needed.

Let's get painting!

MOUNTAIN RAZZLE-DAZZLE

Bob Ross for Kids
Materials Needed:

Kid Liquid White
Kid Landscape Brush
Kid Phthalo Blue
Kid Fan Brush
Kid Titanium White
Kid Bright Red
Kid Painting Knife
Kid Sap Green
Kid Landscape Brush
Kid Van Dyke Brown
Kid Cadmium Yellow
Kid Liner Brush

1 Cover the canvas with Kid Liquid White using the Kid Background Brush. Before it dries, use the same brush and Kid Phthalo Blue stroking side to side starting at the top of the canvas.

Pause **10** minutes

Remember Marta, every painting is going to be different, and that's what makes it great.

Tip

Keep your palette flat on the table while painting.

But Bob, I'm a little nervous to start. What if I make a mistake?

2 Use the Kid Fan Brush loaded with Kid Titanium White to make the clouds. Turn the brush in a circular motion.

3 Mix Kid Phthalo Blue and Kid Bright Red to make dark purple. With the edge of the Kid Painting Knife, shape the mountains using dark purple.

4 Use the Kid Background Brush to blend the mountains down before they dry.

Pause **10** minutes

5 Use the Kid Painting Knife edge loaded with Kid Titanium White to highlight the right side of each mountain peak.

"Let's put a few little highlights in here, just to make them little rascals just sparkle in the sun."

6 Mix Kid Titanium White with a small amount of Kid Phthalo Blue. Use this light blue on the edge of the Kid Painting Knife to add shadows to the left side of the mountain.

7 Paint a foothill at the bottom of the mountain using a mix of Kid Sap Green and Kid Phthalo Blue on the Kid Landscape Brush.

Mountain Razzle-Dazzle

8 Pull down reflections using Kid Sap Green and Kid Phthalo Blue with the Kid Landscape Brush.

Marta, we don't make mistakes, we just have **happy accidents.**

Tip Load your brush by gently dabbing into the paint, don't grab too much!

You mean, **even if the clouds look crooked . . .**

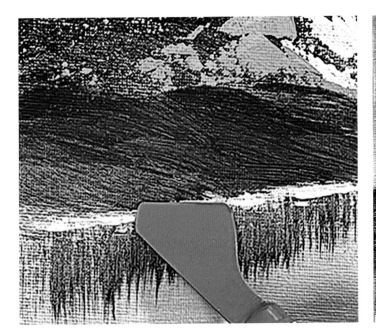

9 Use the edge of the Kid Painting Knife and Kid Titanium White to make a waterline at the bottom of the foothills.

10 Mix Kid Sap Green and Kid Phthalo Blue together to make a dark green. Use the Kid Fan Brush to tap in evergreen trees.

11 Use the mix of Kid Sap Green and Kid Phthalo Blue on the Kid Landscape Brush to paint bushes under the trees.

Pause **10** minutes

MOUNTAIN RAZZLE-DAZZLE

12 Add trunks to the trees with Kid Van Dyke Brown on the edge of the Kid Painting Knife.

. . . or my mountains are shaped like Mr. Moosey's squiggly antlers?

Tip

If your brush gets too dirty while you're painting, a nice rinse in your cup of water every now and then will keep your colors fresh from step to step.

13 Use a mix of Kid Cadmium Yellow, Kid Sap Green and a little Kid Titanium White to tap highlights on the evergreens with the Kid Fan Brush.

14 Use the same Kid Yellow-Green-White mix to add highlights to the bushes with the Kid Landscape Brush.

15 Tap colorful mixes of Kid Bright Red, Kid Cadmium Yellow, and a little Kid Titanium White on some bushes with the Kid Landscape Brush. Finally, use the Kid Liner Brush and any color to sign your painting!

SCENIC SNOWY SUMMIT

Bob Ross for Kids Materials Needed:

Kid Liquid White
Kid Background Brush
Kid Prussian Blue
Kid Bright Red
Kid Painting Knife

Kid Landscape Brush
Kid Titanium White
Kid Van Dyke Brown
Kid Fan Brush
Kid Liner Brush

1 Use the Kid Background Brush to cover the entire canvas with a thin even coat of Kid Liquid White. Proceed to Step 2 before the canvas is dry.

2 Use the Kid Background Brush and Kid Prussian Blue with a small amount of Kid Bright Red to paint the sky area. Start at the top of the canvas working back and forth. This color does not have to go all the way to the bottom of the canvas.

Marta, you can do anything on this canvas. If painting does nothing else, it should make you happy.

Oh Bob! Now I know I can do it! I'm really excited to paint.

Tip

Easy does it with tree highlights. It's tap-tap-tap, not smash-smash-smash!

3 Mix Kid Prussian Blue and Kid Bright Red to make a dark purple. Using a small roll of paint on the Kid Painting Knife, shape the peaks of the mountains. Before the paint dries, use the Kid Landscape Brush to blend the mountain color down to form the body of the mountain. Allow the paint to dry before moving to the next step.

4 Load a small roll of Kid Titanium White onto the Kid Painting Knife. Create highlights to the right side of each mountain peak by allowing this small roll of white to travel down the slope.

5 Mix a little of the purple color used for the mountain into Kid Titanium White to make a light purple shadow color for the peaks. Use a small roll of the light purple color on the Kid Painting Knife on the left side of each peak. Once the shadows and highlights have dried on your mountain, proceed to the next step.

Pause **10** minutes

6 Use Kid Prussian Blue and Kid Bright Red to make a dark purple color. This color will be used to form the dark bush and tree shapes. Load the Kid Landscape Brush with the dark color. Push up on the brush to form rounded bush shapes filling the bottom of the canvas.

7 With a clean Kid Landscape Brush, highlight the top bush shapes. Load the Kid Landscape Brush with Kid Titanium White and push up gently to highlight each bush. The lower bushes will be highlighted later.

To create a "small roll" of paint on the edge of the Kid Painting Knife, flatten some paint on your palette, then scrape the blade across the paint. See! Small roll!

8 Mix a dark brown color using Kid Prussian Blue, Kid Van Dyke Brown, and Kid Bright Red. Use the Kid Fan Brush, pulling down to form a tree trunk. Use the Kid Liner Brush and the dark brown color to paint smaller branches on the tree.

9 Use a small roll of Kid Van Dyke Brown on the Kid Painting Knife to add brown bark to the main trunk of the tree.

10 Use the dark purple color from step 6 to touch dark leaves on top of the tree branches with the Kid Landscape Brush.

11 Use a small roll of Kid Titanium White on the edge of the Kid Painting Knife to touch highlights onto the trunk of the tree. Also, use the Kid Liner Brush and Kid Titanium White to add small bits of snow to the branches of the tree.

12 Highlight the tree using a clean Kid Landscape Brush and Kid Titanium White. Gently touch to add snowy highlights on top of the dark leaves of the tree.

Did you ever think you could just take a great big old brush and make all these beautiful little trees? You really can!

13 Add highlights to the bushes on the bottom of the canvas using the Kid Landscape Brush and Kid Titanium White. Allow the highlights to dry before adding small touches of pink to the snow covered bushes. A small amount of Kid Bright Red added to Kid Titanium White will make a light pink color. Sign your painting using the Kid Liner Brush and a color of your choice.

FALL CABIN ESCAPE

Bob Ross for Kids Materials Needed:

Kid Liquid White	**Kid** Phthalo Blue	**Kid** Painting Knife
Kid Background Brush	**Kid** Landscape Brush	**Kid** Fan Brush
Kid Cadmium Yellow	**Kid** Bright Red	**Kid** Sap Green
Kid Van Dyke Brown	**Kid** Titanium White	**Kid** Liner Brush

1 Cover the canvas with Kid Liquid White using the Kid Background Brush. Before it dries, add Kid Cadmium Yellow to the same brush for the canvas middle, then Kid Cadmium Red for the top, and Kid Van Dyke Brown for the bottom.

Pause **10** minutes

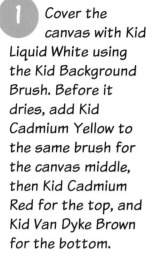

2 Tap happy tree shapes along the sides of the canvas using the Kid Background Brush and Kid Van Dyke Brown.

3 Paint bushes and grassy ground areas at the bottom of the canvas using a mix of Kid Van Dyke Brown and Kid Phthalo Blue.

Pause **10** minutes

4 Use the Kid Landscape Brush with Kid Bright Red, Kid Cadmium Yellow and a little bit of Kid Titanium White to tap highlights on the happy trees and bushes.

5 Using Kid Van Dyke Brown on the edge of the KId Painting Knife, make a cabin shape.

6 Highlight the roof of the cabin with Kid Bright Red on the edge of the Kid Painting Knife. Add a door using the edge of the Kid Painting Knife using a mix of Kid Van Dyke Brown and Kid Phthalo Blue, then outline with a roll of Kid Titanium White on the Kid Painting Knife.

Tip You can move mountains, rivers, trees, you can determine what your world is like!

I can't wait to get started, Bob! And I'll invite **Peapod the Pocket Squirrel** to paint along too!

7 Paint the path to the cabin using Kid Titanium White and Kid Van Dyke Brown on the Kid Fan Brush.

8 Tap grass onto the lower portion of the painting using Kid Sap Green and Kid Titanium White on the Kid Landscape Brush.

FALL CABIN ESCAPE

9 Add fence posts and birds to your painting using the Kid Liner Brush and Kid Van Dyke Brown.

You really can learn to be creative as you paint.

I'm ready to dream up an awesome nature scene on my canvas, Bob.

Tip Twist and twirl the hairs of the liner brush in the paint to make it nice and pointy.

10 Use the Kid Liner Brush and any color to sign your painting. You're a real artist.

SPRINGTIME MAGIC

**Bob Ross for Kids
Materials Needed:**

Kid Liquid White
Kid Background Brush
Kid Landscape Brush
Kid Titanium White
Kid Fan Brush
Kid Sap Green
Kid Phthalo Blue
Kid Van Dyke Brown
Kid Painting Knife
Kid Cadmium Yellow
Kid Bright Red
Kid Liner Brush

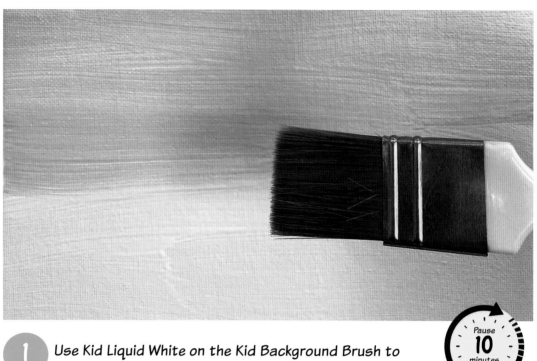

1 Use Kid Liquid White on the Kid Background Brush to cover the canvas. Before it dries, use Kid Phthalo Blue on the same brush to paint the sky by brushing back and forth.

Pause **10** minutes

Tip Happy little trees™ means dropping in dark shapes **without trying to make them perfect.**

The true joy of painting is when you share it with other people, Oliver. **Just let your imagination go.**

I like to share, **Bob.** I'm going to put a cabin in my painting so you and all my friends can visit.

2 Use the Kid Landscape Brush and Kid Titanium White to tap in cloud shapes in the sky.

3 Load the Kid Fan Brush with Kid Sap Green to shape the evergreen trees.

Pause **10** minutes

4 Paint bush shapes using a mix of Kid Sap Green and Kid Phthalo Blue on the Kid Landscape Brush.

5 Add trunks to the evergreen trees using Kid Van Dyke Brown on the edge of the Kid Painting Knife.

SPRINGTIME MAGIC

6 Highlight evergreens with a mix of Kid Cadmium Yellow, Kid Sap Green and a little Kid Titanium White on the Kid Fan Brush.

I knew you could do it. If you learn from anything you try, Trevor, then it's a good day.

Tip Use just the corner of the fan brush for evergreen trees.

Trees are my favorite, Bob. And Funny Bunny here loves **happy trees** too, and flowers.

"Let's make some nice little clouds that just float around and have fun all day."

Pause 10 minutes

7 Highlight the bushes using Kid Titanium White and Kid Bright Red to make a pink on the Kid Landscape Brush.

8 Paint small flowers using the Kid Liner Brush with Kid Titanium White. Also use Kid Titanium White and Kid Cadmium Yellow for more flowers. Kid Phthalo Blue and Kid Titanium White will make blue flowers.

9 Add stems to the flowers using Kid Sap Green and Kid Titanium White on the Kid Liner Brush. Sign your name using the Kid Liner Brush and any color you choose.

SURFING AT SUNSET

Bob Ross for Kids Materials Needed:

Kid Liquid White	**Kid** Landscape Brush
Kid Background Brush	**Kid** Painting Knife
Kid Cadmium Yellow	**Kid** Titanium White
Kid Bright Red	**Kid** Fan Brush
Kid Phthalo Blue	**Kid** Van Dyke Brown
Kid Sap Green	**Kid** Liner Brush

1 Use Kid Liquid White on the Kid Background Brush to cover the canvas. Before the canvas dries, still using the Kid Background Brush, paint the lower right corner with Kid Cadmium Yellow. Then add Kid Bright Red on the Kid Background Brush to paint the middle of the canvas. Using the same brush, add Kid Phthalo Blue to the upper left corner of the canvas to complete the sky.

Pause **10** minutes

The sky can be so colorful Bob, like the feathers Birdman flaps when he's feeling upbeat.

Isn't that fantastic? I don't try to understand everything in nature, I just look at it and enjoy it.

Tip Your sky might look different, but there are **no mistakes, just happy accidents™**.

2 Paint the bottom of the canvas to make water, using Kid Phthalo Blue and Kid Sap Green on the Kid Landscape Brush.

 3 Make wave water lines using the edge of the Kid Painting Knife with Kid Titanium White and Kid Phthalo Blue on it.

4 Mix Kid Phthalo Blue, Kid Bright Red, and Kid Cadmium Yellow together to make a dark color. Use the Kid Fan Brush to paint a land area in the lower right corner.

 5 Use the same dark color again on the Kid Fan Brush to pull down palm tree trunks.

Pause
10
minutes

 Paint the palm branches with the Kid Fan Brush using the dark color.

"Anything that you try and you don't succeed at, if you learn from it, it's not a failure."

7 Add a little Kid Titanium White to the dark color on the Kid Fan Brush to highlight the palm branches.

8 Now make sand! Tap-tap-tap using the Kid Landscape Brush and a mix of Kid Titanium White and Kid Van Dyke Brown.

9 Use the Kid Liner Brush and some dark green color to add grasses on the land and sign your name with a color of your choice.

DREAMING OF SNOW

Bob Ross for Kids Materials Needed:

Kid Liquid White
Kid Background Brush
Kid Bright Red
Kid Phthalo Blue

Kid Titanium White
Kid Fan Brush
Kid Landscape Brush
Kid Liner Brush

1 Use Kid Liquid White on the Kid Background Brush to cover the canvas. Before it dries, use a small amount of Kid Bright Red on the same brush to make a pink circle in the center of the canvas.

Success with painting leads to success with many things. **Do you agree, Trevor?**

Tip Use just the corner of the fan brush for evergreen trees.

You bet, Bob. Painting gives me extra confidence in my school work, sports, and cooking class too!

"Painting should be one of those things **that brightens your day.**"

2 Use Kid Phthalo Blue on the Kid Background Brush to paint around the Pink circle.

Pause **10** minutes

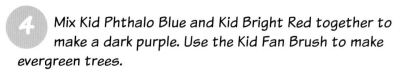

3 Tap soft tree branches along the edges of the canvas using a mix of Kid Titanium White and Kid Phthalo Blue on the Kid Background Brush. Then, using only Kid Phthalo Blue on the same brush, paint darker bushes along the bottom of the canvas.

4 Mix Kid Phthalo Blue and Kid Bright Red together to make a dark purple. Use the Kid Fan Brush to make evergreen trees.

Pause **10** minutes

5 Use the same dark purple on the Kid Landscape Brush to tap dark bushes along the bottom of the canvas.

6 Add highlights to the evergreen trees using Kid Titanium White on the Kid Fan Brush. Then use KId Titanium White on the Kid Landscape Brush to highlight the bushes.

7 Use Kid Titanium White on the Kid Fan Brush to make snow covered land under the bushes. Use the Kid Liner Brush and your dark purple color to paint sticks and twigs in the snow.

"And the more that you paint, the more that you're able to visualize . . . you really can learn to be creative as you paint. It's like anything else, it just takes a little practice."

8 Finally, rinse off your Kid Liner Brush and use Kid Titanium White to add snow on the sticks and twigs and sign your name with a color of your choice.

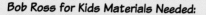

Bob Ross for Kids Materials Needed:

Kid Liquid White
Kid Background Brush
Kid Bright Red
Kid Prussian Blue
Kid Sap Green
Kid Van Dyke Brown
Kid Fan Brush
Kid Titanium White
Kid Painting Knife
Kid Liner Brush
Kid Cadmium Yellow

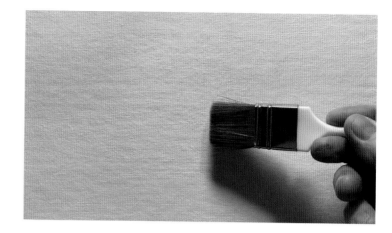

We just show you how, but you make the decisions. When you have this much power, you have to make big decisions.

Tip

You have unlimited power here, you can do that. You can do anything on this canvas, anything.

1 Using the Kid Background Brush, cover the entire canvas with a thin even coat of Kid Liquid White. Before it dries begin painting the sky and water.

2 Use the Kid Background Brush and Kid Bright Red to paint the center portion of the canvas with a back and forth stroke. Now, paint the upper portion of the sky by adding Kid Prussian Blue to the same brush to create a purple color. Without cleaning the brush, use Kid Prussian Blue and a very small amount of Kid Sap Green to paint the water in the lower portion of the canvas.

3 With a clean Kid Background Brush, paint the sandy beach area at the bottom of the canvas using Kid Van Dyke Brown using a back and forth motion.

Pause
10
minutes

4 Mix Kid Prussian Blue and Kid Bright Red to make a dark purple. Use the Kid Fan Brush to sketch in the wave. Copy the shape carefully from the photograph.

5 Load a clean Kid Fan Brush with Kid Titanium White and a small amount of Kid Prussian Blue. Paint the small portion of water to the left of the main wave by gently sliding the Kid Fan Brush from side to side. This will make tiny waves behind the main wave.

6 Now, use the Kid Fan Brush with the same white-blue mix in step 5 to create the water rolling over the top of the wave. Use slightly curved angled strokes from left to right.

7 Still using the Kid Fan Brush, mix a tiny amount of Kid Sap Green into the same white-blue mix used in step 6. This pale white, green, and blue mixture will be used to lighten the area in the middle of the wave by using the Kid Fan Brush in a circular motion.

8 Using the same color, add foam patterns onto the middle portion of the wave using curvy motions to create movement in your wave.

Pause **10** minutes

9 Use a small roll of Kid Titanium White on the edge of the Kid Painting Knife to make a layer of foam laying on the beach. Slide the blade of the knife back and forth in a sawing motion.

Isn't that fantastic? I knew you could do it!

10 Underline the foam on the beach by using the Kid Liner Brush loaded with Kid Prussian Blue and Kid Bright Red. Also add dark purple foam patterns on the center portion of the wave for more detail.

CRASHING OCEAN WAVES

11 Tap the Kid Background Brush in a small amount of Kid Titanium White. Then, tap along the top and bottom edge of the wave to create the splash of the wave. The splash follows the purple sketch of your wave.

12 Use Kid Van Dyke Brown on the Kid Liner Brush to draw a small star on the beach. Use the same brush and color to fill in the starfish shape. Also, add birds in the sky using a clean Kid Liner Brush and Kid Titanium White.

"You have to have dark in order to show light, just like in life."

13 Add highlights onto the starfish using the Kid Liner Brush with a small amount of Kid Titanium White and Kid Cadmium Yellow. The birds have small tips of a dark purple on the ends of the wings. Use the Kid Liner Brush and any color to sign your painting.

Happy Trees Along a Cabin Path

Bob Ross for Kids Materials Needed:

Kid Liquid White
Kid Background Brush
Kid Cadmium Yellow
Kid Van Dyke Brown
Kid Fan Brush
Kid Titanium White
Kid Prussian Blue
Kid Painting Knife
Kid Liner Brush
Kid Sap Green
Kid Landscape Brush

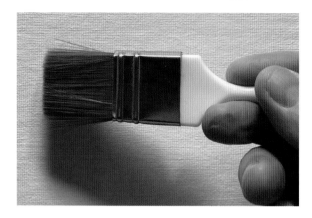

1 Apply a thin, even coat of Kid Liquid White over the whole canvas with the Kid Background Brush. Begin painting the sky in step 2 before the canvas dries.

2 Using the Kid Background Brush, create an oval shape in the middle of the canvas with Kid Cadmium Yellow. Then, without cleaning the brush, use Kid Van Dyke Brown to paint a large oval, starting from the outside edges of the canvas working toward the yellow oval in the center.

Tip Just let your imagination go. You can create all kinds of beautiful effects, just that easy.

This would be a good place for my little squirrel to live.

That's a pretty nice tree for being done that quick!

3 Paint small distant evergreen trees by loading the Kid Fan Brush with a mixture of Kid Van Dyke Brown and Kid Titanium White. Tap down with the Kid Fan Brush to create pointed, distant evergreen trees of different heights.

Pause **10** *minutes*

4 Make a dark brown paint mixture of Kid Van Dyke Brown and Kid Prussian Blue. The color can be mixed by picking up both colors and stirring them together with the Kid Painting Knife. Use the Kid Background Brush to paint the bottom of the canvas brushing side to side. Then, make bush shapes near the center of the canvas by tapping down with the Kid Background Brush.

5 Use the Kid Fan Brush and the dark brown mixture to make more pointed background trees near the center of the canvas. Tap down with a fully loaded Kid Fan Brush.

6 Create larger dark evergreen trees on the right and left sides of the canvas using the Kid Fan Brush loaded with the dark brown mixture. Tap down with the Kid Fan Brush in a side to side motion to form the branches.

Pause
10
minutes

7 Use the Kid Liner Brush to make tree trunks and branches. Dip the Kid Liner Brush into a small amount of water and roll the brush through the dark brown paint. Pull up or down with the Kid Liner brush to make thick tree trunks and slim branches.

8 Mix Kid Sap Green with a very small amount of Kid Titanium white to make a light green color. Load the Kid Landscape Brush with the green color, and tap down to make grasses at the base of the dark evergreen trees. Also, create bushes next to the grassy area by tapping down with the Kid Landscape Brush loaded with the light green color. Tap in rounded shapes to form the bushes.

9 If necessary, mix up more dark brown paint using Kid Van Dyke Brown and Kid Prussian Blue. This color will be used to make Bob Ross's cabin. Use the Kid Painting Knife to form the cabin with a small roll of the brown paint on the edge of the knife.

10 Once the cabin is dry, outline the shape of the cabin with a mixture of the dark brown and a little bit of Kid Titanium White on the Kid Liner Brush. Make boards on the front and side of the cabin by loading a small roll of the light brown mixture on the Kid Painting Knife. Using the small edge of the knife, form shingles on the side of the roof with the light brown mixture. Make a doorway using the small edge of the knife and the dark brown. Outline the doorway with the light brown on the Kid Liner Brush.

Pause **10** minutes

11 Tap in additional grasses using the Kid Landscape Brush loaded with a mixture of Kid Sap Green and a small amount of Kid Titanium White. Add bushes on the lower left and right corners of the canvas using the Kid Landscape Brush. Tap down to create the bushes with a mix of the light green and a small amount of Kid Cadmium Yellow. A small path area to the cabin can be made by sliding back and forth with a small amount of light brown on the Kid Fan Brush.

12 Sign your painting with any color and the Kid Liner Brush.

Winter Mountain Waterfall

Bob Ross for Kids Materials Needed:

Kid Liquid White
Kid Background Brush
Kid Prussian Blue
Kid Bright Red
Kid Fan Brush
Kid Titanium White
Kid Painting Knife
Kid Van Dyke Brown
Kid Sap Green
Kid Landscape Brush
Kid Fan Brush
Kid Cadmium Yellow
Kid Liner Brush

1 Apply a thin, even coat of Kid Liquid White over the entire canvas with the Kid Background Brush. Begin painting the sky and water in the next step before the canvas dries. The brush does not need to be cleaned before the next step.

Pause **10** minutes

2 Starting at the top of the canvas, paint the sky using the Kid Background Brush loaded with Kid Prussian Blue. Use back and forth strokes to cover the sky area about half way down the canvas. Then, use a mixture of Kid Prussian Blue and Kid Bright Red to paint the lower portion of the canvas.

3 Using the Kid Fan Brush, paint clouds in the sky with Kid Titanium White. The clouds can be formed by turning the brush in a circular motion. Pay attention to the top shape of each cloud. Allow the paint to dry for a few minutes before adding additional white to highlight the clouds.

4 Using the Kid Painting Knife, mix a combination of Kid Prussian Blue and Kid Bright Red. Stir the color until it makes a very dark purple color. Now, using a small roll of the dark purple on the edge of the Kid Painting Knife, form the mountain peaks.

5 Before the paint dries, blend the dark mountain color down with a clean Kid Background Brush. This will form the body of the mountain. Let this dry before moving to the next step.

Pause 10 minutes

6 With a small roll of Kid Titanium White on the Kid Painting Knife, highlight the right side of each mountain peak. Hold the knife very lightly as you follow down the slope of each peak.

7 Mix a small amount of Kid Prussian Blue into Kid Titanium White to make a shadow color that will be used for the left side of the mountain peaks. Use a small roll of this light blue color on the edge of the Kid Painting Knife, pulling down and to the left side of each peak.

8 Once the mountain dries, make a dark color by mixing Kid Prussian Blue, Kid Van Dyke Brown, and Kid Sap Green together in equal parts. This color will be used to paint the bushes and trees at the bottom of the mountain.

9 Load the Kid Landscape Brush with the dark color and tap down to create bush and tree shapes of various sizes. Then, pull a little of the dark color down to create reflections on the surface of the water.

"I look forward to seeing you again. Happy Painting, God bless, my friend . . ."

10 Using the Kid Fan Brush loaded with the dark color, create little evergreen trees by pushing lightly up while traveling down the tree. Clean the Kid Fan Brush in water and dry it with a paper towel. Now, make a highlight color for the evergreen trees using a combination of Kid Sap Green, Kid Prussian Blue, and a little bit of Kid Titanium White. Gently tap the highlights on each evergreen tree. Be careful not to cover all the dark color of the trees.

Pause 10 minutes

11 Mix a small amount of Kid Van Dyke Brown and Kid Titanium White to make a waterline color that will be used on the edge of the Kid Painting Knife. Using a back and forth motion, create a thin waterline under the land.

12 Make a very dark brown color with Kid Prussian Blue and Kid Van Dyke Brown. This will be the color used to paint the rock cliffs on each side of the waterfall.

13 Load the Kid Landscape Brush with the dark brown, and pull down at an angle to form the tops of rock cliffs that will be on each side of the waterfall. Leave a space between the two rock formations for the waterfall. Now, using a clean Kid Fan Brush loaded with Kid Titanium White, pull down to create a waterfall. Leave space under the waterfall for a small pond.

Painting is like anything else, Kim, **it just takes a little practice.**

That's true, Bob. My paintings get better and better the more times I try.

14 Using the Kid Landscape Brush loaded with the dark brown mixture, pull down to form rocks on both the left and right side of the waterfall. Continue to paint and form the rock cliffs on both side of the waterfall. A small pond will be left unpainted just under the waterfall.

15 Highlight the rock cliffs using a color combination of Kid Van Dyke Brown and a very small amount of Kid Titanium White on the Kid Landscape Brush. Paint the tops of the rock cliffs, as well as lower rock formations on the cliffs by gently pulling down with the Kid Landscape Brush using the light brown color. The corner of the Kid Fan Brush can be used to form smaller rocks at the base of the cliffs along the water's edge.

16 Use a dark color made by mixing Kid Prussian Blue, Kid Van Dyke Brown, and Kid Sap Green to create dark bushes along the top and sides of the rock cliffs on both sides of the waterfall. Use this same dark color on the Kid Fan Brush to paint a large evergreen tree on the top right hand side of the waterfall. Gently push up on the Kid Fan Brush while traveling down the tree.

17 Using a combination of Kid Van Dyke Brown and a small amount of Kid Titanium White on the edge of the Kid Painting Knife, make a trunk for the large evergreen tree.

Pause **10** minutes

18 Once the tree trunk dries, highlight the large evergreen tree with a combination of Kid Sap Green, Kid Cadmium Yellow, and a small amount of Kid Titanium White.

19 Highlight the bushes on top and sides of the cliffs using the Kid Landscape Brush and the same color used to highlight the evergreen tree.

20 Using a clean Kid Landscape Brush and a very small amount of Kid Titanium White, tap a little splash at the base of the waterfall. Load the Kid Fan Brush with a small amount of Kid Titanium White and use a side to side motion to paint ripples and small splashes on the surface of the pond at the base of the waterfall.

21 Sign your painting with a color of your choice on the Kid Liner Brush.

TRANQUIL DESERT EVENING

1 Cover the entire canvas with a thin, even coat of Kid Liquid White using the Kid Background Brush. Before the canvas dries, use the Kid Background Brush to paint a diagonal strip of Kid Bright Red in the center of the canvas. Then, add Kid Cadmium Yellow to the same brush to make a diagonal strip below the Kid Bright Red. Wash the Kid Background Brush, and then load it with a mixture of Kid Prussian Blue and Kid Bright Red. Paint the area at the top of the canvas with this dark purple color.

These things live right in your brush Kim, all you have to do is shake them out.

Tip You can do anything you want to do. This is your world.

I tap **shining stars** into the sky to gaze up at!

2 Using the Kid Liner Brush, paint a small crescent moon in the dark purple part of the sky with a small amount of Kid Titanium White. Paint a half circle shape and then add a little bit into the center of the moon. Load the Kid Fan Brush with a small amount of Kid Titanium White. Holding the Kid Painting Knife in one hand and the Kid Fan Brush in the other hand, brush the bristles of the Kid Fan Brush against the blade of the Kid Painting Knife toward the canvas. Small spots of white will spray onto the canvas creating little stars in the night sky.

3 Mix a combination of Kid Van Dyke Brown and small amount of Kid Prussian Blue with the Kid Painting Knife. Put a small roll of this dark brown color on the edge of the knife to shape the desert mountain. Before the color dries, blend it down with the Kid Landscape Brush to form the body of the mountain. Allow the mountain to dry before the next step.

4 Mix Kid Cadmium Yellow, Kid Van Dyke Brown, and a small amount of Kid Titanium White. Use a small roll of this gold color on the Kid Painting Knife to create highlights to the right sides of the mountain.

5 Mix Kid Prussian Blue, Kid Bright Red, and a small amount of Kid Titanium White. Use a small roll of this purple color on the Kid Painting Knife to create shadows on the left side of the mountain. Let the canvas dry before proceeding. Mix Kid Van Dyke Brown and a small amount of Kid Titanium White for a final highlight color. Use a small roll of this light brown color on the Kid Painting Knife to create final highlights on the right side of the mountain.

Pause **10** minutes

6 Using a mixture of Kid Sap Green and Kid Cadmium Yellow on the Kid Background Brush, tap in grass along the base of the mountain. Mix Kid Prussian Blue, Kid Van Dyke Brown, and Kid Sap Green. Use the Kid Landscape Brush to tap in dark desert brush shapes near the bottom of the canvas.

7 Use the same dark mixture from step 6 on the Kid Fan Brush to draw cactus shapes growing from the desert brush near the bottom of the canvas.

8 Highlight the cactus using a mix of Kid Cadmium Yellow and Kid Sap Green on a clean Kid Fan Brush.

9 Using the Kid Liner Brush and Kid Sap Green, draw small round cactus shapes. Highlight the rounded shapes using the Kid Liner Brush loaded with Kid Sap Green and Kid Titanium White. You can add cactus blossoms with the Kid Liner Brush and Kid Bright Red.

10 Use a mixture of Kid Cadmium Yellow, Kid Sap Green, and a small amount of Kid Titanium White on the Kid Fan Brush to highlight grasses below the cactus. Push up on the Kid Fan Brush with this light green color to create highlights. When this color dries, add additional shadow colors to the grasses using Kid Prussian Blue, Kid Bright Red, and a small amount of Kid Titanium White on the Kid Fan Brush.

11 Add small desert daisies to the grass area at the bottom of the canvas using combinations of Kid Cadmium Yellow and Kid Bright Red on the Kid Liner Brush. Small stones can be added along the desert path using the Kid Liner Brush and Kid Van Dyke Brown. Highlight the stones with a little bit of Kid Van Dyke Brown and Kid Titanium White.

12 With a small amount of Kid Titanium White and Kid Van Dyke Brown on the Kid Fan Brush, sweep back and forth to highlight the middle of the desert path.

13 Use the Kid Liner Brush and a color of your choice to sign your painting.

MORE ABOUT BOB ROSS

Bob Ross is the soft-spoken guy painting happy clouds, mountains, and trees on television, full of encouraging "you can do its"! Millions of viewers, big or small, still love to watch him paint, with his gentle manner and encouraging words, captivated by the magic that he creates on the canvas.

Born in Daytona Beach, Florida, on October 29, 1942, Bob grew up with his loving mother and brother, Jim. He loved animals and wildlife, and he had so many pets as a kid! When he went to Alaska at age 21, he saw snow for the first time, and this would serve as his painting inspiration for years to come.

Bob Ross has inspired millions, just like you, to pick up a paintbrush! His unique talent and approach makes the intimidating accessible to anyone who wants to try. If you're reading this, you probably already have the vision he intended. Bob Ross opens your eyes to see things about yourself that you hadn't seen before.

The Bob Ross Company was formed in 1981 and is an active behind-the-scenes organization that celebrates almost 45 years of operation, even after the death of Bob Ross in 1995. His company is as strong and dedicated as ever to his philosophy of bringing art to all people, and his painting show continues to air—uninterrupted since 1982—all over the world.